JOHN BAKER

English Stained Glass
of the medieval period

Photographs by
ALFRED LAMMER
with 83 illustrations,
40 in colour

THAMES AND HUDSON

Filmset in Great Britain by Keyspools Ltd, Golborne, Lancashire
Printed in Spain by Heraclio Fournier SA

Introduction

In an age so richly endowed with means of communication, when books are printed and distributed in their thousands, it is understandably difficult to realize the important position which the art of stained and painted glass held as a means of spreading the Christian doctrine in Roman Christendom. It is even more difficult to imagine, from the small quantities of medieval stained glass left in our churches and cathedrals, the enormous number of windows which were produced during the four hundred years between the 12th and the 15th centuries. These were, in many ways, the medieval equivalent of our present cinema or television screens. To the ordinary people, certainly illiterate, and unlikely to have access to missals and psalters in the possession of the rich or scholarly, they provided the most effective means of communicating spiritual truths. Not without reason have the windows been referred to as the 'Poor Man's Bible'. Suger, Abbot of St Denis, one of the first to instal stained glass windows in his church, said: 'The pictures in the windows are there for the purpose of showing simple people who cannot read the Holy Scriptures, what they must believe'. Similarly, an old catechism of the period contains the following question and answer: 'What should one do on entering the church? One should take Holy Water, adore the Blessed Sacrament, then walk round the church and contemplate the windows.'

Also in much the same way as our visual media, medieval stained glass windows provided a very powerful, if veiled, source of propaganda for obtaining gifts or money for the church, or even for winning over new converts to the faith. This is particularly noticeable in those windows dealing with the miracles of the saints. For instance, in exchange for some benefit received from the saint, the recipient promised a gift. Failure to make a donation after the intervention of the saint resulted in speedy and terrible retribution. Most of the windows dealing with the miracles of St Thomas Becket in Canterbury Cathedral come into this category.

The origin of stained glass is not known and has given rise to much speculation. Like most revolutionary steps in art, it was probably the result of a combination of many factors, both technical and aesthetic, together with a reaction against the existing order of things and a desire to alter them. With the gradual change from Romanesque to Gothic, it has been said, 'Walls that had been inanimate became frames for heavenly visions, and no art, throughout the Middle Ages, had such power and prestige with the Christian congregation.' What is perhaps strange is that no evidence exists to show the art in its infancy. The earliest examples remaining today are the five lights, each containing the figure of a prophet, in Augsburg Cathedral in Germany, and part of an 'Ascension' window in Le Mans Cathedral in France. These windows are generally thought to belong to the 11th century, though the figures in Augsburg are by no means primitive and indicate an art form well advanced in design and technique.

The method of filling windows with pieces of coloured glass held together by means of a lead armature bears a striking similarity to that branch of the enameller's art known as *cloisonné*. In the latter form of enamelling, strips of metal are soldered edgeways onto a metal surface to form a design, and the spaces in-between are filled with different coloured glasses by heating in a kiln. This type of enamelling was introduced into France before the end of the 10th century by a colony of Venetians who settled there. It is possible that the idea of making a stained glass window resulted from collaboration between the painter-enamellers and the glaziers. We know that France was already famous for its glaziers from the account in the writings of the Venerable Bede. He records that, as early as the 7th century, they came to England to glaze windows in churches at Wearmouth and Jarrow, and stayed to teach the English their craft. Nevertheless, all such theories remain speculative in the absence of further evidence.

Stained glass was essentially a northern European art form and reached its peak in such beautiful windows as those still to be seen, if rather fragmented, in the cathedrals and smaller churches of France, England, Germany and Austria, dating from the 12th to the 15th centuries. As we have seen, they served a dual function, to decorate the church and to instruct the congregation. It follows that the majority of stained glass windows had for their subject-matter religious themes: scenes from the Old and New Testaments and from the lives and miracles of special saints, figures of saints and prophets, the genealogy of Christ (an especially popular subject), and a host of others. The Bible in use at the time was the Vulgate and this, together with stories of the saints contained in the Golden Legend and various other apocryphal writings, supplied most of the themes for the windows throughout the period covered by this book.

From the 14th century onwards heraldry, and figures of the donors of the windows, played a larger part as subject-matter. The patron eventually became of central importance, as can be seen in the churches at Waterperry in Oxfordshire and Long Melford in Norfolk, and in the chapel in Merton College, Oxford, where the figure of the donor occurs no less than twenty-three times. After the invention of the printing press in the 15th century, other sources of design became available. Dutch and German woodcuts had a very powerful influence on glass painting between the Gothic and Renaissance periods. The large output of engravings based on the paintings of Raphael and other Italian painters led to the spread of their designs, which were copied or freely adapted by glass painters. The results were seen in the many roundels, painted on white glass often embellished with yellow silver stain, that are found in both secular and religious buildings. By this time the art of stained glass had become moribund and remained so until its attempted revival in the 19th century.

Once his subject was decided on, how did the master glazier set about making a window? Our knowledge of the methods used by the medieval glass painters comes mainly from a treatise on the arts in general, compiled by a monk, Theophilus, in the 10th century. Using a small sketch design, which may either have been prepared by the master glazier himself or obtained from one of the illuminators of manuscripts, the glass painter made a full-size working drawing of the window, with a heavy black or red line, on a whitened table top. This cartoon, as it would now be called, included all the details of heads, hands and drapery, as well as the disposition of the lead armature. Different colours were indicated by means of a letter. Having chosen the coloured sheet of glass, the painter laid it over the drawing; the individual piece was then obtained by drawing a red-hot iron round the shape required, after starting a crack by dropping water or – more probably – spitting on it. The resulting rough piece was then grosed away round the edges with a notched iron until the correct shape and size had been obtained. The notches on the back of the modern glass-cutter are a vestige of this medieval grosing iron and are put there for the same purpose.

When all the shapes had been cut they were laid out over the drawing ready for the painter to trace onto the surface of the glass the details of the design, which were seen on the drawing beneath. This he did with an enamel made from copper or iron oxide, mixed with a flux of finely pulverized soft glass and ground with a medium of gum and water, wine, or urine. When all the painting was complete, the pieces of glass were laid out on an iron plate previously covered with a fine layer of ash or quicklime, and fired in a simple kiln. This firing followed every fresh application of paint.

With the firing complete, it remained only to join all the pieces together by means of thin strips of lead of an 'H' section, to smear the joints with suet or resin and to solder them together. When one side was finished the panel was reversed and the other side soldered. The final operation was to force some form of waterproof mastic between the leaves of lead and the glass to make the whole panel watertight. Strips of lead were also soldered to various points on the panel to help secure it to the fixing bars.

Two more technical discoveries complete this account of the craft during the medieval period. Early in the 14th century it was found that, by applying a solution of silver salt to the surface of the glass and firing it, the glass was stained a yellow colour varying from a pale lemon-yellow to a deep orange, almost ruby, depending upon the strength of the solution used and the firing temperature. The solution was applied to the outside surface of the glass, and it revolutionized the art of stained glass.

The second innovation, the process of abrasion, dates from the 15th century. The coloured layer or 'flash' superimposed on the thickness of white glass was removed by grinding it away with an abrasive such as whetstone and water. This made possible two colours, white and red, on the same piece of glass, and with the addition of silver stain, three colours were employed. The technique was to prove invaluable to those concerned with making heraldic windows, where some of the shields had very complicated designs on a very small scale.

The range of yellows obtained from the use of silver salt were the only colours introduced by the artist himself into a stained glass window. All the coloured glass used was obtained from glass-makers in the form of sheets or slabs, the colour being obtained by the addition of metallic salts into the molten glass. Much of the variation we find in the colours of the early windows was probably due to other substances present in the metal salts they used. Those glasses coloured throughout their entire thickness were known as 'pot-metal'. Those which had the thin layer of coloured glass known as 'flash' superimposed upon a thicker layer of white glass were referred to as 'flashed glasses'.

Until late in the 16th century very little glass was made in England, and this small output was all white. Most glass was imported from the Continent through the Merchant Adventurers and the Hanseatic League. Generally speaking, the glass used in the north of England came from Germany and that used in the south was imported from Normandy.

These, then, were the methods and materials used by the medieval glass painters, with little or no change, during the four hundred years covered by this book. But if there were no changes in the craft itself, there were very definite changes in style and approach. Unfortunately for the historian these did not occur suddenly. There was always a degree of overlapping and any attempt to classify the different periods of glass painting must necessarily be arbitrary. One thing only seems to be certain. From the 14th century onwards there was a slow but continuous move towards naturalistic representation, which finally reached its peak in the 16th century. The spirit which had inspired English stained glass artists for three centuries seems to have withered, and this decline was further accelerated by the employment of foreign artists, mostly Germans or Flemings, to carry out large-scale commissions, such as King's College Chapel, Cambridge, and Henry VII's Chapel at Westminster. These influences and, later, the effect of the Reformation officially brought the making of religious stained glass windows in this country to an end.

This book draws attention to some of the finest examples of medieval stained glass. They are all, so far as it is possible to be certain, English, but this does not mean that I consider them to be better or worse than their European counterparts. I do believe, however, that they have not always been as greatly appreciated, or as carefully preserved, as they might have been. In Canterbury at the present time, much money and labour are being expended in trying to preserve for as long as possible some of the finest windows of all time. This kind of assistance needs to be extended to all those cathedrals and churches which have made a contribution to this most beautiful art form before their windows have deteriorated beyond repair.

No reproduction can give the same satisfaction and excitement as seeing the actual window. The translucency, the most important quality associated with a stained glass window, is missing. By concentrating on large-scale details, however, instead of trying to record whole windows, the actual technique of the glass painter can be studied and compared at leisure. Some of the windows illustrated can be better viewed in the photographs than in their original setting, as many of them are inaccessible without scaffolding. No attempt has been made to cover the whole field of stained glass, but the selection has been designed to show as completely as possible the characteristics of each of the main periods of glass painting. The choice is a personal one, for which I make no apology. I hope there will be many who will want to share it.

Notes to the Plates

12th–13th CENTURIES

Border Details 13th century. Canterbury Cathedral. North side of Trinity Chapel.　　　　PLATE 1
Details from windows 1, 4, 6
If nothing else remained, one could appreciate the richness and grandeur of 13th-century windows from the borders which surrounded them, especially in the large churches and cathedrals. Much wider than later borders, with brilliant colour, exquisitely painted detail and elaborately composed patterns of infinite variety, they are perhaps the finest and most typical examples of the art of stained glass ever to be produced.

Adam, Jareth Late 12th century. Canterbury Cathedral　　　　PLATES 2, 3
These large figures, two to each light, originally formed part of a series in the clerestory of the choir and eastern transepts. They depict the Genealogy of Christ, beginning with the figure of Adam, probably surmounted by the Creation of Adam and ending with the figures of Christ and the Virgin. Hardly any of them have escaped the hand of the restorer, but in spite of this they still retain much of their original grandeur. They are generally accepted as being the oldest windows in the Cathedral.

Head in Profile Late 12th century. Perhaps from Rochester. Victoria and Albert Museum, London　　　　PLATE 4
This head bears a striking resemblance to the restored head of Seth, one of the original clerestory figures of Canterbury Cathedral, now in the west window. If it is not the original head of Seth, the latter must have been used as a model by the restorer.

St Eilward leaving Canterbury Early 13th century. Canterbury Cathedral. North aisle of Trinity Chapel　　　　PLATE 5
This panel is one of a series illustrating the story of Eilward of Westoning, who was taken before a magistrate for stealing. He was sentenced to be blinded and mutilated, but was later restored to health by the intercession of St Thomas; on being healed he gave alms to the poor. As there is some reference to leprosy in the inscription, it remains possible that this panel may well belong to an entirely different narrative.

The Parable of the Sower Early 13th century. Canterbury Cathedral. North choir aisle, second window　　　　PLATE 6
One of two scenes of the Sower, this figure is somewhat archaic in design, but it is well composed with a very subtle use of colour for the landscape. The panel is still flanked as it originally was by the Old Testament 'types'. On the left are the rich men of this world, on whom the life of the seed is choked, and on the right, the three righteous men – Daniel, Job and Noah – representing the seed sown in good ground.

The Burial of Nurse Britonis Early 13th century. Canterbury Cathedral. North aisle of Trinity Chapel　　　　PLATE 7
The twelve windows in Trinity Chapel, six on each side, are believed to have contained panels relating to the Life and Miracles of St Thomas Becket, Archbishop of Canterbury. Very little of the original glass remains, most of it having been destroyed during the Reformation. The remaining panels illustrate subjects from the miracles believed to have taken place after his murder, either through his direct intercession or by the healing powers of his blood. This detail is taken from the first scene in the story of the plague which struck the house of Sir Jordan Fitz-Eisulf of Pontefract; Nurse Britonis is the first victim of the plague. The death of Jordan's little son follows three days after the nurse. The pilgrims from Canterbury bring Holy Water, which Jordan pours into the mouth of the dead child. He places gold coins, which are to be given as a mid-Lent offering, in the hands of the child. The little boy recovers but the parents forget the offering. A leper is bidden by the Saint to warn them of their forgotten promise and the consequences of their neglect. The warnings are ignored and the knight's eldest son dies, his servants become afflicted, and the knight and his wife become ill. Finally, the knight fulfils his promise to the Saint, and he, his wife and their youngest son are restored to health.

Visit of the Queen of Sheba to Solomon Early 13th century. Canterbury Cathedral. North choir aisle,　　　　PLATE 8
second window.
Detail showing camels

PLATE 9   *Noah in the Ark* 12th century. Canterbury Cathedral. North choir aisle
Noah, at the open window of the ark, receives the returning dove with the olive-branch.

PLATE 10   *The Cure of the Maniac* 13th century. Canterbury Cathedral. North aisle of Trinity Chapel
This panel probably belongs to the story of Henry of Fordwich, a dangerous lunatic, who was brought before the Saint to be cured of his affliction. An interesting feature of the window is the foliated pattern scratched from a matt applied to the blue background. It is a common feature of German and Austrian glass of the 13th century, but is rarely found in English glass until it eventually became a characteristic feature in the 14th century.

PLATE 11   *The Virgin Mary* Late 12th century. Canterbury Cathedral. North window of the corona.
Detail from a Jesse window
This window has had a curious history. In a lecture to the Archaeological Institute in 1848, Charles Winston referred to it, together with part of another in York Minster, as being some of the oldest stained glass in the country. There is also a coloured tracing of it, dated 1848, in the Victoria and Albert Museum in London. Sometime later the panel disappeared from the Cathedral and was not seen again until it was returned under the terms of the will of the late Dr Philip Nelson, a well-known collector and authority on stained glass, in the late 1950s.

PLATE 12   *The Burning of Sodom and the Escape of Lot* Early 13th century. Canterbury Cathedral. North choir aisle
The panels which make up windows 2 and 3 in the north choir aisle are all that remain of those which once filled the twelve windows in the choir aisles and two eastern transepts. The lights were divided up into medallions. The central vertical column contained illustrations from the New Testament, each panel having on either side another with a scene from the Old Testament foreshadowing it. They are generally known as the 'Theological' windows. The detail shown here is the figure of Lot's wife, looking back on the ruins of burning Sodom. The use of white glass for her figure, instead of the more usual brownish-pink, is intended to show that she is already turning into a pillar of salt.

PLATES 13, 14, 15   13th century. Westminster Abbey. Jerusalem Chamber, north window
The north window of the Jerusalem Chamber contains seven panels of 13th-century glass which may have come from any window in the eastern part of the Abbey except Henry VII's Chapel. They were probably placed in their present position when the chamber was restored in the 17th century. These panels probably provide the closest parallel between English and French glass of the period.

The Stoning of Stephen
The Legend of St Nicholas of Myra
This panel formed part of a series illustrating the story of the little boy and the golden cup taken from the Golden Legend (see the 16th-century version of the same story in Hillesden Church, Plate 79). Decay of the glass and careless re-leading have made it difficult to distinguish the various figures clearly.

Beheading of John the Baptist
The head of St John is a modern restoration. The repulsive face given to the figure of the executioner is very typical of the medieval period, when everything was done to convey to the spectator the full significance of the story and the people taking part, so that faces could become almost caricatures.

PLATE 16   *Female Figure with a Book* 13th century. White-Notley Church, Essex
This fragment now set in a small window in the vestry of the church may have been part of the east window of the original apse. When the present vestry was built on the foundations of a ruined chapel, the glass was found embedded in a Saxon priest's tombstone, in the north arch of the chancel.

PLATE 17   *The Last Judgment* 15th century. St Mary's Church, Fairford, Gloucestershire. West window of the window.
Detail showing the head of Christ

PLATE 18   *Adoration of the Magi* 13th century. Church of the Nativity of Our Lady, Madley, Herefordshire. East window. Detail showing the Madonna and Child

PLATE 19   *Figure of St Paul* 13th century. Lincoln Cathedral. South aisle, east window.
Detail

The ancient glass remains in Lincoln Cathedral rank as second in importance in England and, as with most stained glass of this early period, their authorship is unknown. Compared with the glass in Canterbury Cathedral, the glass enamel used for painted details has worn very badly and much of it has disappeared altogether, probably due to being insufficiently fired. The colour of these windows is lighter and gayer than one usually finds in glass of this period and the drawing is very vigorous (see Plates 21, 22).

The Martyrdom of St Catherine 1210–25. West Horseley Church, Surrey. East window   PLATE 20
With the exception of the small Madonna and Child in Compton Church, this is probably the oldest stained glass in Surrey. The east window contains two small roundels of early 13th-century glass, one of St Catherine and the other showing St Mary Magdalen washing Christ's feet. It can be appreciated how much skill and patience went into the making of these early medallions when it is realized that in this small roundel, only twelve inches in diameter, there are 109 separate pieces of glass.

Head of Christ 13th century. Lincoln Cathedral. North aisle, east window.   PLATE 21
Detail

Return of the Prodigal Son 13th century. Lincoln Cathedral. South-west transept, south window.   PLATE 22
Detail of a man's head

14th CENTURY

The Nativity 14th century. East Hagbourne Church, Berkshire. North aisle   PLATE 23
This panel combines the rich colour of the 13th century with characteristic details of the 14th century. The simple painted canopy, the diapered background and the narrow block borders are all typical of the latter period. Only two panels remain and little seems to be known about them.

Annunciation to the Shepherds Latter half of the 14th century. Victoria and Albert Museum, London   PLATE 24
This roundel provides a good illustration of the use of silver stain, a discovery dating from the early part of the century, and of a more sentimental approach to the subject-matter: quite distinct from the objective, slightly austere outlook of the previous century. The figures have more movement and the style of drawing indicates a transition from the earlier glass to the greater realism of the 15th century which was to follow.

Virgin and Child 14th century. Eaton Bishop Church, Herefordshire. East window.   PLATE 25
Detail
It is interesting to compare the rather more general treatment of this subject with the more unusual approach shown in Plate 26 (see also Plates 41, 42)

Virgin and Child 14th century. Church of St John the Baptist, Fladbury, Worcestershire. North   PLATE 26
window of the vestry
The figure of the Virgin is powerfully drawn, highly conventionalized, with the utmost economy of line. The colour used is very cool in tone and the whole panel has an extraordinarily 'modern' look. There is a similar panel in the nearby church of Warndon, which undoubtedly came from the same workshop, if not the same artist, but is in a more advanced state of decay.

Figures of a Knight and of the Prophet Joel 14th century. Tewkesbury Abbey, Gloucestershire. North-   PLATES 27, 28
east clerestory of the apse (see also Plates 29, 31)
In the north-east and south-east windows of the apse are large figures of the prophets and knights of the De Clare and De Spencer families. Above these figures are soaring, richly coloured canopies, while below, on a background of quarries, are set their shields of arms. The prophets are similar in their drawing but not in their colouring to some of the figures in Gloucester Cathedral. All the figures are set against diapered backgrounds painted in reserve.

Head of the Prophet Joel 14th century.   PLATE 29
Detail from Plate 28

PLATE 30   *Kneeling Woman* 14th century. Tewkesbury Abbey, Gloucestershire. East window
The seven lights of the east window contain all that remains of a window depicting the Last Judgment. The figure of a naked kneeling woman against a blue background, painted in reserve with a seaweed pattern, is contained in the extreme right-hand bottom panel, and may have represented the donor.

PLATE 31   *Figure of a Knight* 14th century.
Detail from Plate 27

PLATE 32   *Figure of a Prophet* 14th century. Church of the Nativity of Our Lady, Madley, Herefordshire. East window
The east window is filled with the remains of 13th- and 14th-century glass, which probably at one time filled the rest of the church. Among these remains are three panels from what must have been a very beautiful Jesse window. Two of the figures are kings, the one illustrated is of Ezechiel, the only remaining prophet. On the scroll behind the figure is inscribed in Lombardic capitals: [EZE] CHIEL PRO.

PLATE 33   *Figure of a Prophet* 14th century.
Detail from Plate 32

PLATES 34, 35   *St Edward the Confessor and a Bishop* 1325–33. Wells Cathedral, Somersetshire. Choir clerestory, south side
The windows of Wells Cathedral are considered to be among the finest examples of 14th-century glass in England. The comparatively small quantity of blue glass used in these windows gives a general effect of rich, warm colour. The figures are set beneath high canopies and enclosed by block borders, some with a fleur-de-lis and others with a lion as motif.

PLATE 36   *St Catherine* Early 14th century. The Priory Church, Deerhurst, Gloucestershire. South aisle, west window
The most popular and most typical window of the 14th century consisted of a figure or subject set beneath a canopy. The canopies were similar to those engraved on the brasses or sculpted on the tombs of the period, and ranged from the simplest arch-form with crocketed gable, finishing with a foliated finial, to the more elaborate constructions to be seen at Tewkesbury Abbey and Eaton Bishop church. Sometimes, as in this window, they were merely painted on white glass. St Catherine is standing in the characteristic 'S' pose against a rich, striated, ruby background. She holds in her hand the wheel of her martyrdom.

PLATE 37   *Head of a Man* 14th century. Marsh Baldon Church, Oxfordshire. East window.
Fragment
This head is particularly interesting, since it is painted on the brownish-pink glass of the 13th century, but the hair is silver-stained, a characteristic feature of the following century.

PLATE 38   *St Anne Instructing the Virgin* 14th century. Marsh Baldon Church, Oxfordshire. East window
St Anne wears a headdress and wimple of the period, while the Virgin has a simple chaplet of flowers. The beautiful drawing of the hands is especially to be noted.

PLATE 39   *Saints Thomas Becket and Thomas Cantilupe* Early 14th century. St Mary's Church, Credenhill, Herefordshire. South-east window
This window has remained intact in spite of orders issued during the Reformation that all such works should be destroyed. An interesting feature is the use of the Bishop's family name 'Cantilupe', instead of 'Herefordensis'. He was canonized in 1320 and although it is unlikely that the glass was put in before that date, it must have been soon after, during the episcopate of Thomas Charlton, 1327. In order to distinguish the one from the other, the artist has made use of the family name.

PLATE 40   *Sir James Berners* Late 14th century. St Mary's Church, West Horsley, Surrey. North side of chancel
The kneeling figure of the knight, a patron of the church, is set against a quarry background decorated with bands of yellow stain and small yellow flowers. He wears the armour of the late 14th century. He was beheaded in 1388, which places the window right at the end of the 14th century. Beneath the figure is an inscription, showing the change in letter forms from Lombardic to black-letter type. The white glass used for the figure has a distinctive greenish hue and may have come from Chiddingfold, one of the few centres of glass-making in England at that time.

Head of St Michael c. 1317–21. Eaton Bishop Church, Herefordshire. East window. PLATE 41
Detail from Plate 42

St Michael Weighing a Soul c. 1317–21. Eaton Bishop Church, Herefordshire. East window PLATE 42
The east window of this church contains some of the loveliest stained glass to be seen in England. Rich
colour, beautiful drawing and composition, all contribute to give a high standard of excellence. This is
one of the earliest examples of the use of silver stain, and is probably of the 'Westminster' school of
glass painting. The figure of St Michael stands in the curious 'S' pose, holding the scales in his right
hand. In the one pan is the 'Soul' while in the other was probably the figure of a devil, now obliterated.
St Michael is surmounted by a richly coloured, tall canopy. There are windows very similar in style in
the nearby churches of Brinsop and Mamble.

Head of a Horse 14th century. Merton College, Oxford. PLATE 43
Fragment from a window in the library
This beautifully drawn head must have formed part of a larger window, now destroyed. The trappings
are silver-stained and the glass has a silvery grey quality often found in the glass of this period.

Medallion of a Pelican in her Piety c. 1400. Victoria and Albert Museum, London PLATE 44
This was probably one of the roundels set against a quarry background which were popular in both
secular and religious buildings. The bird is painted on white glass against a deep ruby background.

Figure of a Gentlewoman 14th century. Church of St Mary the Virgin, Waterperry, Oxfordshire. North PLATE 45
window of the nave
During the early 14th century grisaille windows continued much as they were in the latter part of the
previous century, but with two main differences. Cross-hatching used in the backgrounds was
abandoned, and foliage was treated more naturalistically. The plant forms used were recognizable as
belonging to definite plants, the oak, vine, ivy, and were no longer confined within definite shapes but
were allowed to trail round them or intertwine with them as in the window illustrated. This and the
adjoining light contain figures of a gentleman and his wife, who were probably the donors of the
window. They wear richly coloured robes and are placed against a simple quarry background
decorated with a trailing pattern of acorns and oak leaves in silver stain.

Figure of the Donor 1298–1311. Merton College Chapel, Oxford. North side of the chapel PLATE 46
There are seven three-light windows on each side of the chapel. With the exception of two at the south-
east end, each window has in the centre light a small panel with a figure of one of the prophets, standing
under a low architectural canopy, against a blue or ruby background. In the side lights, and in a similar
setting to the centre figure, is the kneeling figure of the donor of the windows, Henry de Mamesfeld, a
Chancellor of the University and later Dean of Lincoln. This was probably the first appearance of a
donor in a window and was to prove a characteristic feature of this and later periods of glass painting.
Although it is obvious that a conventionalized portrait has been painted, it is interesting that in some of
the lights he appears with a beard, while in the majority he is clean-shaven. One of the earliest and best
examples of this type of window.

15th CENTURY

Head of an Archbishop c. 1410. Canterbury Cathedral. West window of the water tower. PLATE 47
Detail
This is a beautifully drawn head, rendered with fine lines and light stippled matt. So delicate is the
modelling that, unless seen against a clear sky, most of it is lost. Although one can admire the subtle
painting, it is questionable whether such delicacy of treatment was best suited to the glass painter. This
same fineness of detail was often employed in windows placed so high up in the church that they could
never be seen in detail by the naked eye. In the early glass, when the windows were intended to instruct
as well as to decorate, the broad treatment of detail, as in the clerestory figures in Canterbury, enables
them to be seen quite clearly from the ground. But with the spread of knowledge, this aspect of glass
became less important, and the subtleties of the picture painter slowly infiltrated into the glass-painter's
art.

The Assumption of the Blessed Virgin 15th century. Church of Saints Peter and Paul, East Harling, PLATE 48
Norfolk. East window

In the 'subject' windows of the 15th century small panels were set beneath canopies and arranged in rows across the lights. A fine example of this type of window is in Wrangle Church, Lincolnshire, but perhaps the most perfect set is seen in the church at East Harling in Norfolk. The subject of the fifteen scenes depicted in this window is 'The Joys and Sorrows of the Blessed Virgin Mary'. They are set beneath simple canopies painted on white glass and silver-stained. Here the Virgin is seen ascending to Heaven attended by angels, a crown above Her head.

PLATE 49   *Figure of a Knight* 15th century. Church of Saints Peter and Paul, East Harling, Norfolk. East window. Detail
The kneeling figure of Sir Robert Wingfield, the principal donor of the window, who died in 1480. He wears round his neck the Yorkist collar of alternate suns and roses. The scroll above his head bears the inscription: FILI REDEMPTOR MUD [I DEUS] MISERERE NOBIS.

PLATE 50   *Angel* 15th century. Church of Saints Peter and Paul, East Harling, Norfolk.
Detail from Plate 48

PLATE 51   *The Resurrection* 15th century. Church of Saints Peter and Paul, East Harling, Norfolk. East window. Detail showing a soldier
All the figures in these panels are beautifully drawn and have the quality associated with early German woodcuts, but from a comparison of the drawing of the hands in several of the panels it is obvious that a number of different artists were responsible for the painting, not all of them of the same skill and assurance.

PLATE 52   *Pieta* 15th century. Church of Saints Peter and Paul, East Harling, Norfolk. East window.
Detail showing the head of the Virgin
The seated figure of the weeping Virgin holds the body of the dead Christ (the upper half has been restored). Behind Her stand the figures of St Mary Magdalen and St John.

PLATE 53   *Boy Harrowing* 15th century. Victoria and Albert Museum, London
Originally in Cassiobury Park, this is one of a series portraying the Labours of the Months. They are all beautiful compositions, painted with a vigorous line and scratched-out matt and the use of much silver stain. An example of secular glass very popular in the 15th century. These early ones, dating from the first part of the century, do not show the influence of Flemish glass painting, which came later.

PLATE 54   *Roundel with a Hen* 15th century. St Peter's Church, Ketteringham, Norfolk
The five-light east window contains a number of fine shields and two roundels, and also a rebus on the names of Thistleton and Henry. The one illustrated shows a hen with the letters REY on a scroll. They are painted on white glass, and there is strong yellow silver stain on the bird.

PLATE 55   *Sleeping Soldier* 15th century. Church of St Mary and St Nicholas, Wrangle, Lincolnshire.
Detail from Plate 56

PLATE 56   *The Resurrection* 15th century. Church of St Mary and St Nicholas, Wrangle, Lincolnshire. North aisle, east window
The right-hand light of this window contains (at the top) the Resurrection and (beneath) the Ascension of the Virgin Mary. The side towers of the canopy have eagles and lions alternately standing on stone shelves, which may be the symbols of the Evangelists. There are also small figures of angels, each holding a book and with the left hand raised in blessing. Compare with the soldier from the same subject (Plate 51).

PLATES 57, 58   *The Last Judgment* 15th century. St Mary's Church, Fairford, Gloucestershire. West window of the nave.
Details showing blue fiend and satan
The lower half of this window contains the remains of a 'Doom' or 'Last Judgment' window. This was a splendid theme for the medieval glass painter and one which gave him every opportunity to display his power of imagination and sense of the dramatic. In the centre of this seven-light window is St Michael, weighing the souls. Beneath him the graves yield up their dead. In the three lights to the left the good are being received into Paradise by St Peter and the angels who defend them from the devils. In the three right-hand lights the lost souls are being carried into eternal torment by fiends, some being driven, some

on the backs of the demons, while one who appears quite unconcerned by his fate is being transported in a wheelbarrow. Although ecclesiastical and royal figures are shown among the saved, it is not uncommon for such eminent men to be included among the damned, an indication that the evil-doer, whatever his station in life on earth, would receive his deserts in the next world. The figure of satan occupies the whole of one light and is an astonishing composition in red, with very little other colour used. This is another example of the story and drama taking precedence over everything else: it was a warning to the spectator of the shape of things to come.

St Mary Salome, Zebedee and Children 15th century. Holy Trinity Church, Goodramgate, York. East PLATE 59
window.
Detail of child with bird

St Mary Cleopas, Alphaeus and Children 15th century. Holy Trinity Church, Goodramgate, York. East PLATE 60
window
The groups of married saints seen in this plate were favourite subjects of the York glass painters, according to one authority. There seem to be two reasons for their popularity. The increased veneration shown to the Virgin, and therefore to Her Mother St Anne, in the 15th century, was the first. The second was the appeal they must have made to the married lay-folk, who regarded them as a veiled criticism of the monastic orders. Celibate monks, who regarded the unmarried state as one of the principal Christian virtues, tended to fill windows with celibate saints and virgins, but were often guilty of the immoral practices which they condemned in others. Marriage, in their view, was only to be resorted to by those without the gift of continency.

St William in Exile c. 1421. York Minster Choir. North transept, St William of York window. PLATE 61
Detail showing the head
This is one of the finest heads in the window and shows the York school of glass painting at its highest peak of development both in composition and draughtsmanship, though the window bears evidence of being painted by more than one hand and varies in quality.

Adam Digging 15th century. Church of St Mary Magdalen, Mulbarton, Norfolk. East window PLATE 62
All the glass in the east window originally belonged to Martham Church, which still has remains of the series.

Figure of God 15th century. Church of St Mary and St Clement, Clavering, Essex. Tracery light, east PLATE 63
window
The glass in the east window is in a very incomplete state, as a result of damage caused at the end of the last century. It is very rare to find the Almighty shown in the form of a human.

Seraph 15th century. Church of St Mary and St Clement, Clavering, Essex. North aisle, tracery light, PLATE 64
east window
Angels were another popular subject of the medieval glass painter, usually found in tracery lights, though sometimes, as at Great Malvern Priory, full-size figures appear. Of the nine orders of the heavenly hierarchy, cherubim, seraphim, thrones, archangels and angels are most commonly represented. These angels were usually depicted in one of two ways. In the first type they are shown clad in white robes, often enriched with decoration in silver stain; in the second type they are completely covered with gold feathers, with eyes on their wings rather in the manner of a peacock, and often stand on a wheel. All angels are shown with curly golden hair and white haloes. Sometimes they are shown playing musical instruments or as supporters for heraldic shields.

Figure of Thomas Peyton 15th century. Church of the Holy Trinity, Long Melford, Suffolk. East PLATE 65
window
Originally all the windows in the church contained religious and secular figures of the Clopton family, who were the principal donors. Most of these were destroyed during the 16th and 17th centuries, but the clerestory was left untouched.

Our Lady of Pity or Pieta 15th century. Church of the Holy Trinity, Long Melford, Suffolk. East PLATE 66
window
This subject became popular in England during the 15th century. The Virgin is shown seated on a

decorated throne. In her arms she supports the body of Christ, crowned with thorns and showing on His body the marks of His scourging.

PLATE 67   *Acts of Mercy Window* 15th century. All Saint's Church, North Street, York. North side of the nave.
Detail
The seven corporal acts of mercy were another popular subject of the medieval glass painter. This window contains six of the scenes: feeding the hungry, giving drink to the thirsty, clothing the naked, housing the stranger, visiting the sick, visiting the prisoners. Burying the dead is missing and visiting the prisoners is the one illustrated. The figures have the typical bulbous noses of the York school of glass painting.

PLATE 68   *The Head of King David c.* 1460. Margaretting Church, Essex. East window.
Detail
Jesse windows were not so popular as in the previous century and very few examples have survived. In design they follow closely those of the 14th century. In this window the figures are in pairs, contained within loops formed by the vine, but the general shapes formed by these loops are clumsy, although the colour and treatment of the details is very fine. N. H. J. Westlake, who spent much of his time restoring and studying the window, believed it to be by John Prudde of Westminster, who was responsible for the glass in Beauchamp Chapel, Warwick.

PLATE 69   *Head of the Prophet Zephaniah c.* 1400. Victoria and Albert Museum, London
The three-light window, originally in Winchester College Chapel, contains the figures of St John the Evangelist, St James the Less and the prophet Zephaniah. The head of Zephaniah shows the change in style which began to be more pronounced in this period, a change towards natural appearance. The more conventionalized portraits of the previous centuries were gradually superseded by attempts to show individual character. The heads are always painted on white glass, more modelling is employed, and hands and feet bear a closer resemblance to their natural shape and proportion. There was thus a slow but continuous move towards the three-dimensional modelled figures of the 16th century.

PLATE 70   *God's Covenant with Abraham* 15th century. Great Malvern Priory Church, Worcestershire. South choir aisle of St Anne's Chapel
In spite of having the usual history of destruction and neglect common to most of the cathedrals and churches in England, Great Malvern Priory still retains one of the largest and most varied collections of stained glass to be seen in this country. This is one of the few remaining scenes of the seventy-two which once filled the south clerestory windows of the nave. God appears to the kneeling figure of Abraham and promises that his wife Sarah shall bear him a son, Isaac.

16th CENTURY

PLATE 71   *The Curzon Family* 16th century. Church of St Mary the Virgin, Waterperry, Oxfordshire.
Detail of father with sons
The donor continued to be an important feature in the windows of this period, often shown with his wife and family. They were usually found as in this window, the husband kneeling facing his wife, the sons behind the father, the daughters behind the mother. The figures are set against a quarried background decorated with an interlacing pattern in silver stain.

PLATE 72   *Roundel of a Pieta* 16th century. Victoria and Albert Museum, London
The Reformation, with its revolutionary change in religious opinion, prevented the making of religious windows, and until the end of the century glass painters concentrated upon the production of heraldic or secular windows. These often consisted of roundels set against plain glazed backgrounds. The subjects depicted were sometimes religious and used for private devotion; at other times they consisted of classically inspired scenes or merely scrolls with inscriptions in black-letter type. Skulls were also a favourite motif. This roundel, showing the Holy Women mourning over the body of Christ, may well be of Flemish origin or painted by an Englishman working under Flemish influence.

PLATE 73   *The Head of the Prophet Micah* 16th century. St Mary's Church, Fairford, Gloucestershire. North aisle of nave.
Detail

While the Fairford glass, except for the 'Doom' window, is generally uninteresting in colour and poor in drawing, some of the best examples are to be found in the figures of the prophets which fill the main windows of the north and south nave aisles. The features show a greater knowledge and use of anatomy and the rich robes and in some cases fantastic headdresses of the figures combine to give a thoroughly un-English character to these windows.

The Nativity 1501–02. Great Malvern Priory Church, Worcestershire. North transept   PLATE 74
This window was given to the priory by Henry VII and is the latest of the glass. The four centre lights, in eleven scenes, illustrate the Joys of Mary based on the verses of the Magnificat. The outer lights contain the remains of four large archangels and their bases are the figures of Henry VII, his Queen, the Prince of Wales and three knights. Above the panels is a verse of the Magnificat and below a sentence summarizing the scene. There are no canopies in this window, the cusped heads of the lights being filled with a bust of God, His hands raised in blessing.

The Resurrection 16th century. St Mary's Church, Shelton, Norfolk. North aisle, east window.   PLATE 75
Detail showing the head of Christ
This head is lightly modelled with a stippled matt; the heavy blacks used to accentuate the form give the head the appearance of a photograph taken with a flashlight. The light as a whole is poor in drawing, very little consideration having been given to the distribution of the colour masses, which are too deep in tone for the rest of the composition. Everything has been sacrificed to gain an effect of visual realism, but the result is merely the creation of a bad design. The glass is also very poor in quality.

Bedygfeld Shelton 16th century. St Mary's Church, Shelton, Norfolk. East window, south aisle   PLATE 76
In this two-light window are the figures of the donor, Bedygfeld Shelton, and his wife. They face each other and are both kneeling in prayer. The figures are beautifully painted, the hands and faces delicately modelled with a stippled matt. The window is a fine example of 16th-century glass, but if we accept a stained glass window as a pattern of glass bounded by leads, as in the earlier periods, then these are strictly not stained glass windows, but paintings on glass. The steady move towards three-dimensional rendering of the scene, apparent in the glass of the 15th century, has here reached its climax. The leads in most cases bear little or no relation to the form, and seem to be regarded as a necessary evil. The glass is used as a canvas upon which as realistic a rendering of the figure as possible has been made, colour being used sparingly, and then only to accentuate the visual realism. However much we may admire the window as a painting, it represents the decline of the art of stained glass. With the discovery of glass enamels and their later frequent use, the end was complete.

The Miracles of St Nicholas 16th century. Hillesden Church, Buckinghamshire. East window, south   PLATE 77
aisle.
Detail from the story of the robbers and the Jew. See also Plate 82.

Three Sailors 16th century. Hillesden Church, Buckinghamshire. East window, south aisle.   PLATE 78
Detail from Plate 80

The Miracles of St Nicholas 16th century. Hillesdon Church, Buckinghamshire. East window, south   PLATE 79
aisle.
Boy and the devil
The eight lights in this window show scenes from the Miracles of St Nicholas based on the stories from the Golden Legend. They are very rich in colour, the style of drawing showing a marked Flemish influence. During the feast of St Nicholas's Day, the devil, dressed as a pilgrim, begs alms at the gate of the nobleman's house. The host sends his son to the beggar with food, but the devil entices the boy to the crossroads and there strangles him. He is taken back to the nobleman's house, where, after appeals are made to the Saint, he is miraculously restored to life. The inscription reads: STRANGULAT DEMON PUERUM [PUL] MANTA FERENTEM.

The Miracles of St Nicholas 16th century. Hillesden Church, Buckinghamshire. East window, south   PLATE 80
aisle.
The boy and the gold cup
A rich nobleman, wishing for a son, offered prayers to the Saint, promising, should his wish be granted, that he would have made a gold cup to be consecrated at the altar of the Saint. The boy was born and the nobleman had the cup made, but was so pleased with it that he kept it for himself, having a duplicate

made for the Saint. During the voyage to the church the little boy, while holding the gold cup, fell into the sea and was lost. The second gold cup was offered at the altar of the Saint, but three times it fell to the floor. The child appears holding the first cup and both are offered to the Saint. The inscription reads: CADIT PUERULUS QUEM MOX SALVAT NICHOLAUS.

PLATE 81 *The Miracles of St Nicholas* 16th century. Hillesden Church, Buckinghamshire. East window, south aisle.
Detail of sailors emptying grain
During a time of famine at Myra, a fleet of grain ships bound for Alexandria put into harbour. St Nicholas ordered the sailors to unload the grain, promising that, however much was unloaded, the amount remaining should not be lessened.

PLATE 82 *The Miracles of St Nicholas* 16th century. Hillesden Church, Buckinghamshire. East window, south aisle.
The robbers return the gold to the Jew
One of three panels telling the story of the rich Jew who placed an image of the Saint in his house in the belief that it would protect his goods. Robbers broke into the house and stole everything except the image of St Nicholas. The Jew, in anger, beats the image with his staff. The figure of St Nicholas confronts the robbers and warns them that unless the goods are returned to the Jew they will be hanged. In the scene illustrated, the thieves are seen returning the gold to the Jew, who is then converted to the faith. The detail of this window, especially some of the figures and faces, shows quite a pronounced Flemish influence, the robbers especially looking like characters from a Bruegel painting. They are rich in colour and the modelling of the figures is very powerful.

PLATE 83 *The Arms of Pigott, Quartering Castelline and Walcott* c. 1562. Victoria and Albert Museum, London
An example of the very rich effects to be obtained by the skilful use of silver stain. The proper use of this stain depends upon a number of factors, the type of glass used, the amount and application of the silver salt and, most of all, the control of the firing, which obtains the clear, rich colour seen in this panel. Any shade of yellow, from the pale lemon more often seen in the 14th century, to the deep orange, almost ruby colour in this coat of arms, can be obtained, but to get this depth of colour without 'metalling' the glass calls for great skill in firing. The glass paint has been applied in washes, rather like a watercolour technique, ranging from a pale grey to deep black. The glass was then covered with a thin matt of the glass paint from which were brushed, or scratched with a stylo, the highlights, to give a very dramatic and highly modelled finish.

12th-13th centuries

ON IS · SIC REGES DOMINO CANTM

ALOM : REGINA & RA

14th century

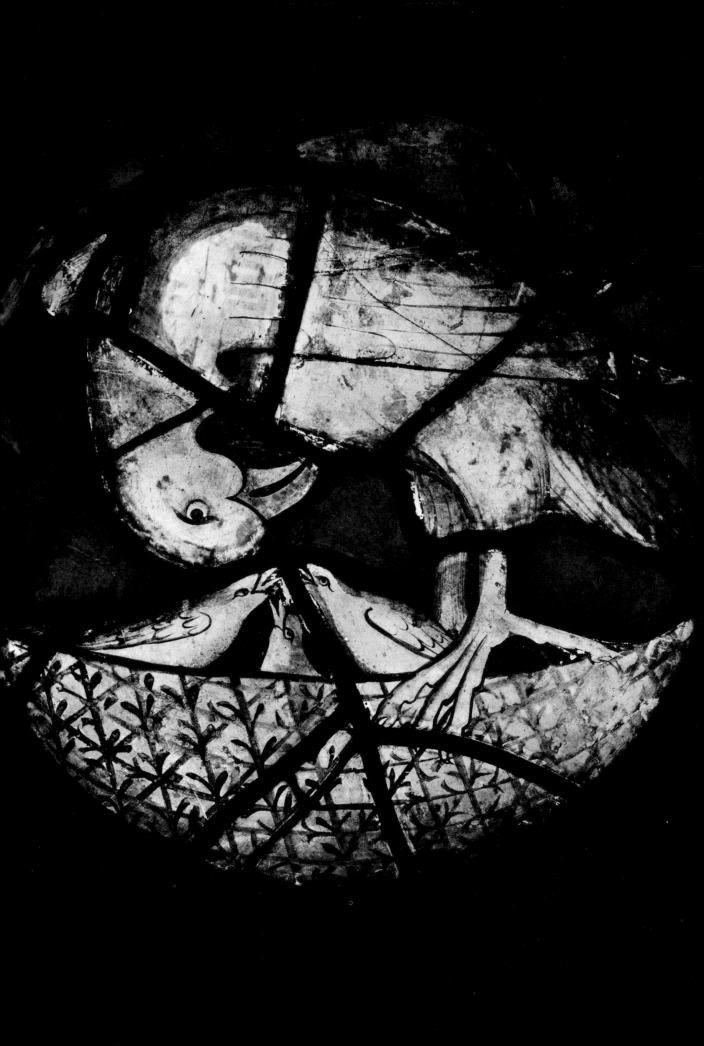

15th century

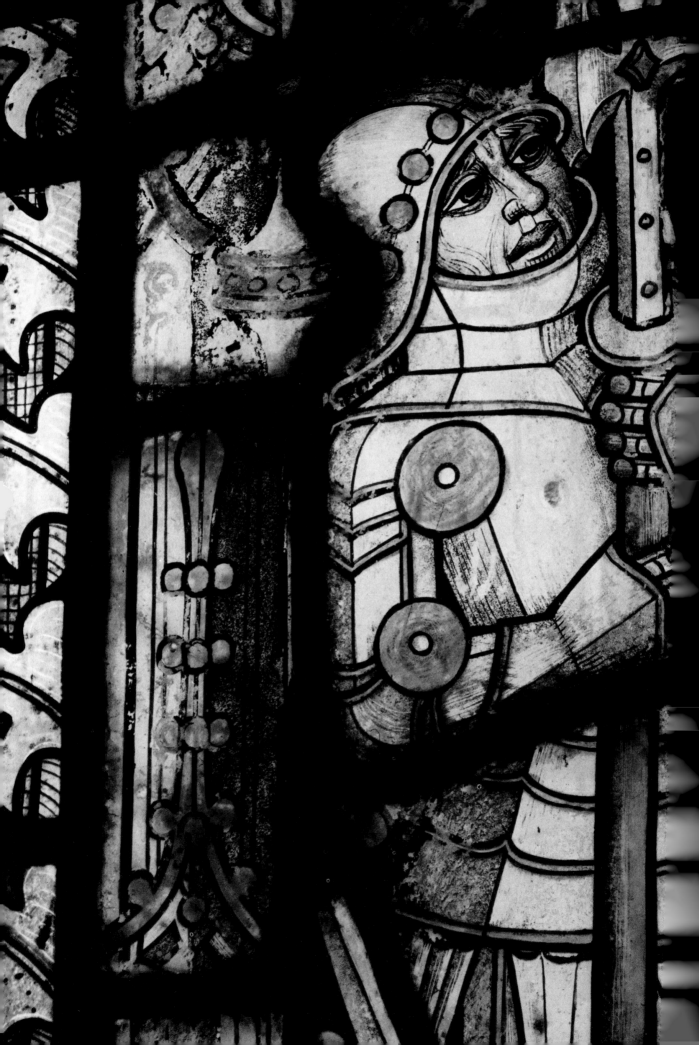

62

Orate p. ã Thomæ Peyton

16th century